W9-ADL-227

The Cuter Book

Cute and easy to make!

ARONZO
ARANZI ARONZO

Table of Contents

White Rabbit: "Hey, look! We made these cute little frogs!"

Brown Bunny: "We made them by following the easy instructions in this book, right?"

White Rabbit: "Right! We made them ourselves!"

Brown Bunny: "Everything is illustrated, so even kids like us can have fun while making them!"

White Rabbit: "I'm pretty bad at making things, but even I had fun!"

Brown Bunny: "What should we make next?"

White Rabbit: "There's so many to choose from! I don't know!"

Brown Bunny: "Yeah, there are just too many cute and cuter things to make in this book, it's hard to decide."

White Rabbit: "The pics are cute. Just looking at them makes me happy."

Brown Bunny: "Right? There are so many pics that simply flipping through the pages is exciting."

White Rabbit: "I know. Since we made these frogs, let's play with them."

Brown Bunny: "Okay!"

White Rabbit: "Ribbit, ribbit, ribbit."

Brown Bunny: "It's fun to play with toys we made ourselves. Ribbit."

Before You Start

Frequently Used Materials and Tools

Scissors
To cut patterns, cloth, felt and thread.

Chalk Pencils
Chalk pencils are used to outline your patterns. Use light pencils for dark fabrics and dark pencils for light fabrics so they stand out. Chalk pencils are useful because you can erase them if you mess up. A simple colored pencil will do if you don't have a chalk pencil.

Felt Fabric
You can use the colors specified in the respective "Materials" sections, or you can use felt in colors of your choosing.
No one will be angry if you use the colors you like!

Embroidery Thread

Used to make eyes, noses and mouths. Also used in cross-stitching.
Use the colors specified in the "Materials" sections or use your own favorite colors.

Sewing Needle
Used when sewing with one embroidery thread. Any size will do. Use what works for you.

Embroidery Needle
For French Knot or Strait Stitches using 3 or 6 threads. It's thicker and has a larger eye than a sewing needle. Use whatever size you like.

Glue
To tack down felt. Either fabric or wood glue is fine.

Tweezers or Toothpick
Used to stuff cotton into narrow parts. A toothpick is useful when applying small amounts of glue.
If you don't have toothpicks, use whatever you have on hand.

Eyes
Use the kind that have pupils that move. Use glue to attach. Craft stores sell them in all sizes. Use whatever size you like.

How to Make Patterns

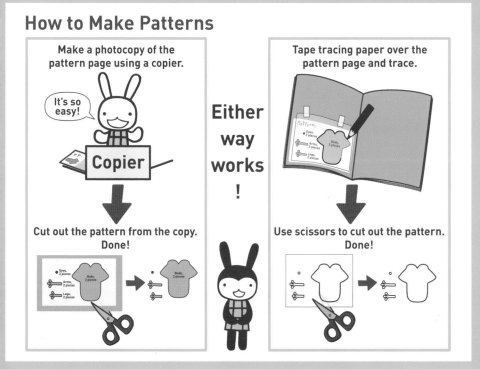

Make a photocopy of the pattern page using a copier.

It's so easy!

Copier

Cut out the pattern from the copy. Done!

Either way works!

Tape tracing paper over the pattern page and trace.

Use scissors to cut out the pattern. Done!

Tracing Patterns onto Felt

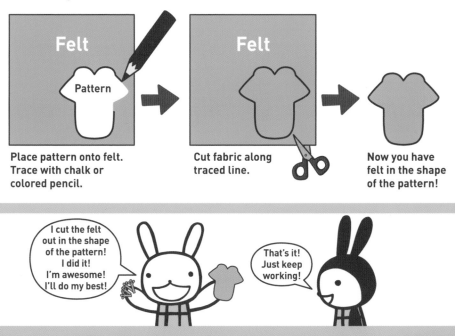

Felt

Pattern

Place pattern onto felt. Trace with chalk or colored pencil.

Felt

Cut fabric along traced line.

Now you have felt in the shape of the pattern!

I cut the felt out in the shape of the pattern! I did it! I'm awesome! I'll do my best!

That's it! Just keep working!

Needles and Thread

Threading 1 strand through your needle: "1 strand."
Threading 6 strands through your needle: "6 strands."

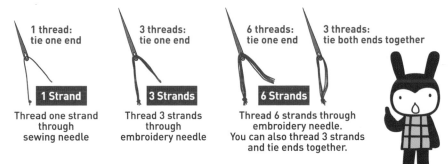

1 thread: tie one end

1 Strand

Thread one strand through sewing needle

3 threads: tie one end

3 Strands

Thread 3 strands through embroidery needle

6 threads: tie one end

6 Strands

Thread 6 strands through embroidery needle. You can also thread 3 strands and tie ends together.

3 threads: tie both ends together

Use **a sewing needle** for 1 strand and **an embroidery needle** for 2 or more strands.
The eye of a sewing needle is very small, so threading more than 1 strand through is tough.

Various Sewing and Stitching Techniques

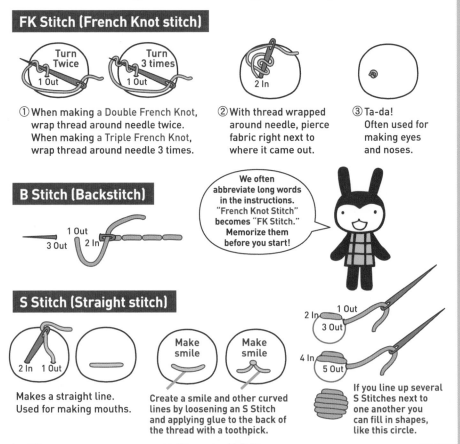

FK Stitch (French Knot stitch)

Turn Twice
1 Out

Turn 3 times
1 Out

① When making a Double French Knot, wrap thread around needle twice. When making a Triple French Knot, wrap thread around needle 3 times.

2 In

② With thread wrapped around needle, pierce fabric right next to where it came out.

③ Ta-da! Often used for making eyes and noses.

B Stitch (Backstitch)

1 Out
3 Out   2 In

We often abbreviate long words in the instructions. "French Knot Stitch" becomes "FK Stitch." Memorize them before you start!

S Stitch (Straight stitch)

2 In   1 Out

Makes a straight line. Used for making mouths.

Make smile

Make smile

Create a smile and other curved lines by loosening an S Stitch and applying glue to the back of the thread with a toothpick.

1 Out
2 In   3 Out
4 In   5 Out

If you line up several S Stitches next to one another you can fill in shapes, like this circle.

How to Add Arms and Legs

Place the felt pieces on top of the illustration to make sure you put the arms and legs in the right places.

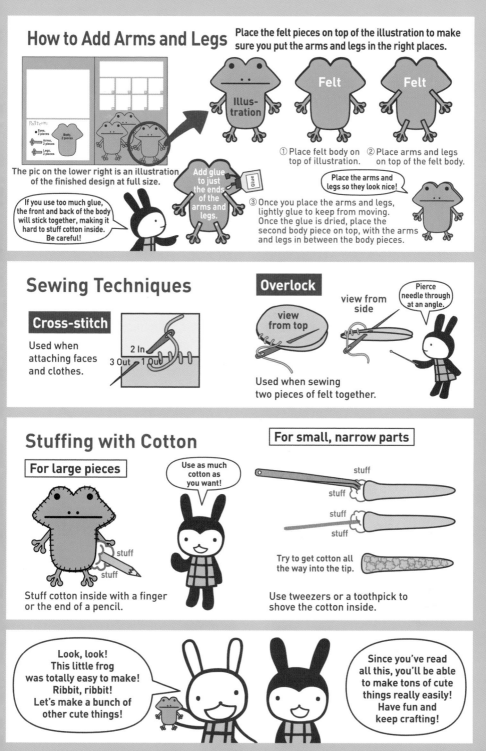

The pic on the lower right is an illustration of the finished design at full size.

Add glue to just the ends of the arms and legs.

If you use too much glue, the front and back of the body will stick together, making it hard to stuff cotton inside. Be careful!

① Place felt body on top of illustration.
② Place arms and legs on top of the felt body.

Place the arms and legs so they look nice!

③ Once you place the arms and legs, lightly glue to keep from moving. Once the glue is dried, place the second body piece on top, with the arms and legs in between the body pieces.

Sewing Techniques

Cross-stitch

Used when attaching faces and clothes.

2 In
3 Out 1 Out

Overlock

view from top

view from side

Pierce needle through at an angle.

Used when sewing two pieces of felt together.

Stuffing with Cotton

For large pieces

Use as much cotton as you want!

stuff
stuff

Stuff cotton inside with a finger or the end of a pencil.

For small, narrow parts

stuff
stuff
stuff
stuff

Try to get cotton all the way into the tip.

Use tweezers or a toothpick to shove the cotton inside.

Look, look! This little frog was totally easy to make! Ribbit, ribbit! Let's make a bunch of other cute things!

Since you've read all this, you'll be able to make tons of cute things really easily! Have fun and keep crafting!

Froggy

1 frog - ribbit.
2 frogs - ribbit ribbit.
3 frogs - ribbit ribbit ribbit.
The more frogs, the more fribbit!

Patterns

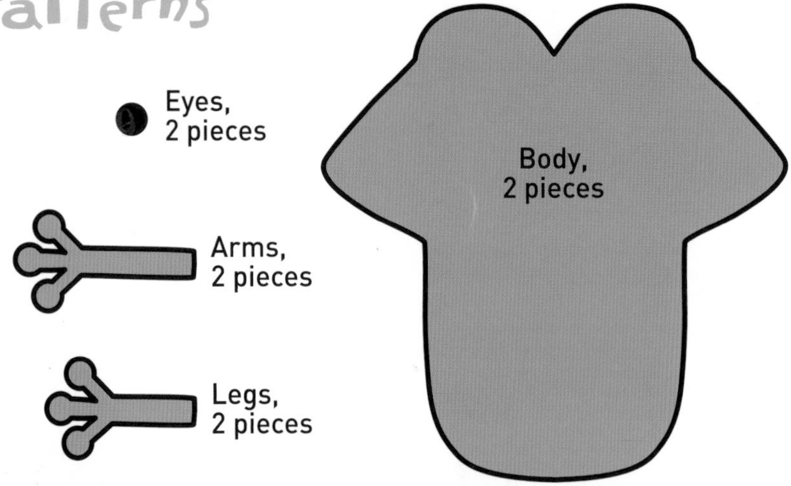

Eyes,
2 pieces

Arms,
2 pieces

Legs,
2 pieces

Body,
2 pieces

Materials

Cotton

Green | Black

Felt

Green
Black

Embroidery Thread

01 Cut felt according to patterns.

02 Cutting out the hands is ribbit hard! Use small, sharp scissors to cut them out!

03 Glue on eyes.

04 Nostrils: Double FK stitch. black thread, 6 strands

05 Mouth: S stitch. black thread, 6 strands

06 Position arms and legs. Lightly glue arms and legs so they don't move. Glue

07 With arms and legs in between, overlock stitch around body. green thread, 1 strand

08 Stuff with cotton, sew shut. Finribbit! green thread, 1 strand

09

Munky

The munkys love to hang out. Make lots and lots of munkys so they can all hang out together! Oui?

Patterns

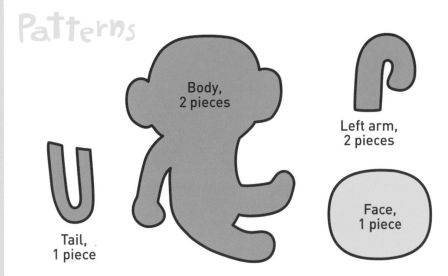

Body, 2 pieces

Left arm, 2 pieces

Tail, 1 piece

Face, 1 piece

Materials

Cotton

Felt
Any brown | Peach

Embroidery Thread
Brown (same as body)
Peach
Brown

01 Cut the felt according to the patterns.

02 Eyes: Triple FK stitch.
brown thread, 6 strands

03 Nose and mouth: S stitch.
brown thread, 6 strands
Stitch like this.
1 Out 2 In 3 Out 4 In 5 Out 6 In
10 In 9 Out 7 Out 8 In

04 Position face.

05 Cross-stitch face onto body.
peach thread, 1 strand

06 Overlock stitch left arm pieces together.
same color thread, 1 strand
to here from here

07 Stuff with cotton.
The arm is narrow, so use tweezers or a toothpick and add cotton a little at a time.
Cotton

08 Affix left arm and tail with glue.
Only use a small amount of glue. If you glue the pieces it makes it easier to sew.
Glue

09 With arm and tail in between, overlock stitch body pieces together.
My arms and legs are narrow, so stuff cotton a little at a time.
same color thread, 1 strand
Sew shut after stuffing.
Done!

10 Our arms fit over the tails!

11 It's fun to hang out!

11

Dharma

This Dharma doll makes your dreams come true.
But you still have to work hard!
Dharma will cheer you on as you work towards
your goal. "Keep up the good work, aye?"

Patterns

Base,
1 piece

Body Stripes,
1 each

Body,
2 pieces

Pupils,
2 pieces

Face,
1 piece

Eyes,
2 pieces

Materials

Cotton

Felt
Red | Peach | White | Black

Embroidery Thread
Red
Black
Peach
White

01 Cut felt according to patterns.

02 Glue eyes onto face, then cross-stitch.
white thread, 1 strand

03 Wrinkles: an S Stitch.
black thread, 6 strands
Glue backs of threads to make cool wrinkles.
Add glue like this, aye?

04 Glue the back of the threads. Give it a peaceful face.
Mouth: S stitch.
black thread, 6 strands

05 Glue the back and curve into a cool mustache.
Mustache: S stitch.
black thread, 6 strands

06 Lightly glue face onto body, then cross-stitch.
peach thread, 1 strand

07 Lightly glue stripes onto body, then cross-stitch.
white thread, 1 strand

08 Overlock stitch body parts together.
red thread, 1 strand
to here↑   from here↑

09 Overlock stitch base to body.
This is hard, aye?
Base
Do your best!
red thread, 1 strand

10 Stuff with cotton, sew shut.
red thread, 1 strand
You can't see my face 'cause this is my back, aye?

11 Glue on just one pupil. Then think of a goal. Work towards that goal daily.

12 When you reach your goal, glue on the other pupil.
By my eye, you did it, aye?

13

Cuddlies

Cuddlies are colorful little bears and bunnies.
Make them in a bunch of colors.
When you line them up they look so cute!
Don't you want to make a ton of them?

Patterns

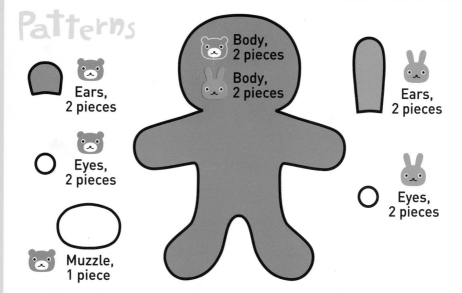

Ears,
2 pieces

Body,
2 pieces

Body,
2 pieces

Ears,
2 pieces

Eyes,
2 pieces

Eyes,
2 pieces

Muzzle,
1 piece

Materials

Cotton

Felt: Any color / White

Embroidery Thread: Black / Same as body

01 Cut felt according to patterns.

02 Cut felt according to patterns.

03 Glue on eyes and muzzle.

04 Pupils: Triple FK stitch — black thread, 6 strands
Nose: Double FK stitch

05 Mouth: S Stitch — black thread, 6 strands
1 Out / 2 In / 3 Out / 4 In

06 Glue on eyes

07 Pupils: Triple FK stitch
Nose: Double FK stitch
Mouth: S stitch — black thread, 6 strands

08 With ears in between, overlock stitch body together. — same color thread, 1 strand

09 With ears in between, overlock stitch body together. — same color thread, 1 strand

10 Stuff with cotton.

11 Sew shut. (Done!)

15

Polar Bear and Cub

A mommy polar bear and cub. They roar, "We're gonna eat you!" They're very friendly. Make both the mom and cub at the same time!

Patterns

Cub ears,
2 pieces

Cub mouth,
1 piece

Cub body,
2 pieces

Bear body,
2 pieces

Bear ears,
2 pieces

Bear mouth,
1 piece

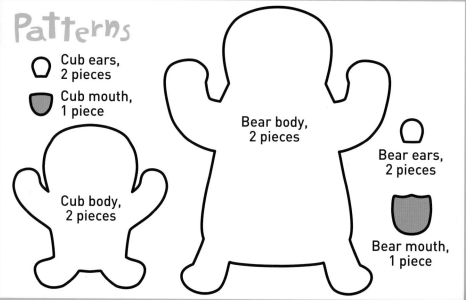

Materials

Cotton

White	Light Brown
Felt

Gray
White
Black

Embroidery Thread

Cut felt according to patterns.
Bear!   Cub!
01

Glue on mouths.
02

Eyes: Double FK stitch.
black thread, 6 strands

Eyes: Double FK stitch.
black thread, 6 strands
03

Nose: S stitch.   Wrinkle: S stitch.
black thread, 6 strands
gray thread, 6 strands

Nose: S stitch.
black thread, 6 strands
04

With ears in between, overlock stitch body together.
white thread, 1 strand
white thread, 1 strand
05

Stuff with cotton and sew shut.
Cub: Done!
Bear: Done!   **06**

17

Happy

Happy is always happy.
Since she's happy,
she always says, "Happy!"
Makes you kinda jealous, doesn't it?

Patterns

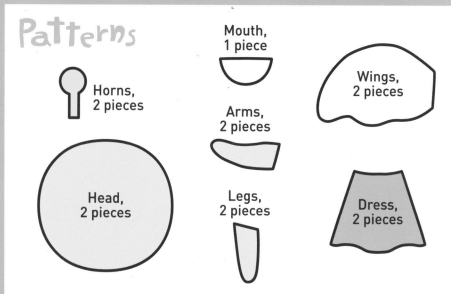

Horns,
2 pieces

Mouth,
1 piece

Arms,
2 pieces

Wings,
2 pieces

Head,
2 pieces

Legs,
2 pieces

Dress,
2 pieces

Materials

Cotton

Felt
Peach | White | Pink | Yellow

Embroidery Thread
Peach
White
Pink
Brown

01 Cut out felt according to patterns.

02 Eyes: Triple FK stitch.
brown thread, 6 strands

03 Lightly glue then cross-stitch on mouth.
Happy!
white thread, 1 strand

04 Place horns.
Happy!
Glue
Lightly glue to keep horns from moving.

05 With horns in between, overlock stitch head together.
Happy!
peach thread, 1 strand

06 Stuff with cotton, sew shut.
Happy!
Cotton
peach thread, 1 strand

07 Place arms and legs.
Glue
Lightly glue arms and legs to keep them from moving.

08 With arms and legs in between, overlock stitch dress together.
pink thread, 1 strand

09 Stuff with cotton, sew shut.
Cotton
pink thread, 1 strand

10 Sew head to dress.
peach thread, 1 strand

11 Lightly glue wing onto back.

12 Cross-stitch on wings.
white thread, 1 strand

13 Done!
Happy!

14 Happy!

Turtlies

The big turtle carries her baby on her back.
And on the baby turtle's back is the baby's baby turtle.
It's kinda confusing. I don't really get it.
Must be hard for the big turtle on the bottom, though.

Patterns

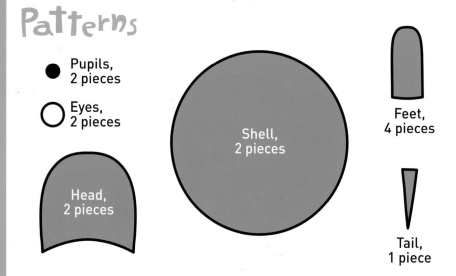

- ● Pupils, 2 pieces
- ○ Eyes, 2 pieces

Head, 2 pieces

Shell, 2 pieces

Feet, 4 pieces

Tail, 1 piece

Materials

Cotton

Felt: Any shade of green · White · Black

Embroidery Thread: Same as turtle

01 Cut felt according to patterns.

02 Glue on eyes.

03 Glue on pupils.

04 Overlock stitch head pieces together.
turtle color, 1 strand

05 Stuff with cotton, sew shut.
turtle color, 1 strand
Cotton

06 Place feet.
Lightly glue feet in place to keep from moving.

07 With feet in between, overlock stitch shell together.
turtle color, 1 strand
Use pins to hold pieces together while sewing.

08 Stuff with cotton.
Cotton
If you use a lot of cotton, the shell will be nice and round.

09 Sew shut.
turtle color, 1 strand

10 Sew head and shell together.
T-Done!
turtle color, 1 strand

11 Make a bunch of Turtlies in all colors!
T-Fun!

12 Make Turtlies in all sizes and stack them up!
You can enlarge or shrink the patterns.
T-Cute!

21

Birdies

They sleep, wake, fly -
baby birds are always busy.
They sing, eat, think - they sure stay busy.
Make baby birds in all kinds of colors!

Patterns

Beak, 1 piece

Body, 2 pieces

Body, 2 pieces

Head, 2 pieces

Tail, 1 piece

Legs, 1 piece

Wings, 2 pieces

Body, 2 pieces

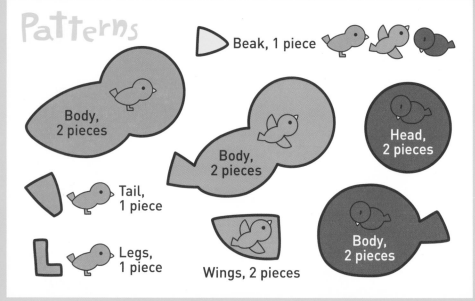

Materials

Cotton

Felt: Any color for birds · Yellow

Embroidery Thread: Brown · Same as birds

---

01 Cut felt according to patterns.

02 Eyes: Triple FK stitch
brown thread, 6 strands
Both sides!

03 Place beak, tail, and leg.
Glue lightly in place to keep from moving.

04 With the parts in between, overlock stitch body together.
Standing bird, done!
same color as body, 1 strand
Stuff with cotton, sew shut.

---

01 Cut felt according to patterns.

02 Eyes: Triple FK stitch
brown thread, 6 strands
Both sides!

03 Place beak and wings.
Glue lightly in place to keep from moving.

04 With beak and wings in between, overlock stitch body pieces together.
Flying bird, done!
same color as body, 1 strand
Stuff with cotton, sew shut.

---

01 Cut felt according to patterns.

02 Eye: S stitch.
Make a sleeping eye.
brown thread, 6 strands

03 Overlock stitch around. Stuff with cotton.
Don't forget the beak!
same color as body, 1 strand

04 Lightly glue head to body.
Sew from back.
same color as body, 1 strand
Sleeping bird, done!

23

Ghost

Ghost comes out to play at night.
This little Ghost loves to scare people,
even though he's not very scary at all.

Patterns

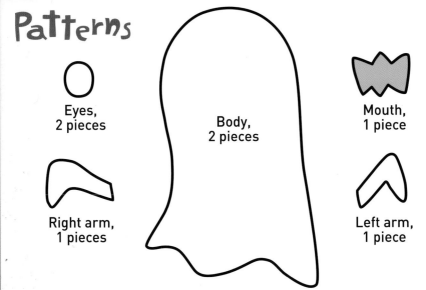

Eyes,
2 pieces

Body,
2 pieces

Mouth,
1 piece

Right arm,
1 pieces

Left arm,
1 piece

Materials

Cotton

Felt — White, Red

Embroidery Thread — White, Black

Black Colored Pencil

01 Cut felt according to patterns.

02 Glue on eyes. "Scary?"

03 Draw around the eye with a black colored pencil or pen.
Hard to see white eyes on a white body, right? So outline in black.
Use a very sharp pencil for a clean line.
They pop now, right?

04 Pupils: Double FK stitch. black thread, 6 strands

05 Glue on mouth. "Scary?"

06 Place arms. Glue on lightly to keep from moving. Glue

07 With the arms in between, overlock stitch around body. white thread, 1 strand

08 Stuff with cotton.

09 Sew shut. "Done!" white thread, 1 strand

10 Try making a bunch of different little ghosts!
See? It's fun to make a lot! Or is it scary?

Eyelash Bunny

Eyelash Bunny always wants to be even more pretty.
Which means that no matter how cute you make her, she's never satisfied. Such a troublemaker.

Patterns

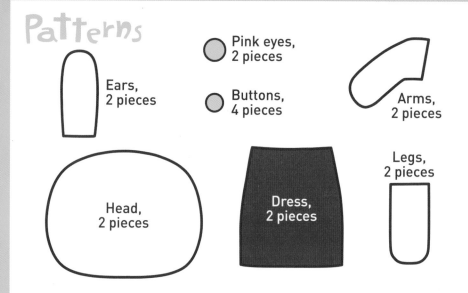

Ears,
2 pieces

Pink eyes,
2 pieces

Buttons,
4 pieces

Arms,
2 pieces

Head,
2 pieces

Dress,
2 pieces

Legs,
2 pieces

Materials

Felt
White | Pink | Red

Cotton

Embroidery Thread
White
Red

Colored Pencil Pink

01 Cut felt according to patterns.

02 Glue on pink eyes.

Glue

03 Pupils: Triple FK stitch.
red thread, 6 strands

04 Eyelashes: S stitch.
red thread, 6 strands

05 Nose: Double FK stitch. Mouth: S stitch.
red thread, 6 strands

06 With ears in between, overlock stitch around head.
white thread, 1 strand

07 Stuff with cotton, sew shut.
Cotton
white thread, 1 strand

08 Place arms and legs.
Glue
Glue in place to keep from moving.

09 With arms and legs in between, overlock stitch around dress.
red thread, 1 strand

10 Stuff with cotton, sew shut.
Cotton
red thread, 1 strand

11 Glue on buttons.
Glue

12 Sew head onto dress.
white thread, 1 strand

13 Color in cheeks and ears with a pink colored pencil. Make me look cute!

14 Done! But I still want to be cuter. What should I do?

27

Snakies

Snakies with flowers on their backs. The flower pattern is what makes them charming. Snakies with big mouths. Their big mouths are also charming.

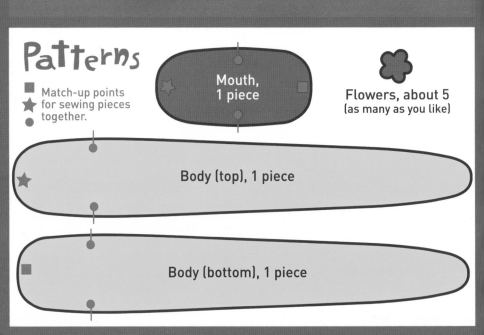

Patterns

■ ★ ● Match-up points for sewing pieces together.

Mouth, 1 piece

Flowers, about 5 (as many as you like)

Body (top), 1 piece

Body (bottom), 1 piece

Materials

Cotton

Felt
- Any color (body)
- Any color (mouth)
- Any color (flowers)

Appx. actual size
● ● 2 pieces
1/4" (6mm) goggly eyes
(sold at craft stores)

Embroidery Thread
Same as body

---

01 Cut felt according to patterns.
Mark pieces with match-up points.

02 Place flowers on body (top).
Put them anywhere!

03 Sew flowers onto body with a double FK stitch in the middle.
same color as body, 6 strands.

04 Match mouth and top body pieces and pin in place.
body (top)
mouth

05 Overlock stitch together.
from here
to here
same color as body, 1 strand

06 Match mouth and bottom body pieces using markings.
mouth
body (bottom)

07 Overlock stitch.
same color as body, 1 strand
to here
from here

08 Match up top and bottom of body.

09 Overlock stitch body together.
same color as body, 1 strand

10 Stuff with cotton, sew shut.
Cotton
The tail is narrow, so use tweezers or a toothpick to stuff cotton.

11 Glue on goggly eyes.
Done!
Glue

12 Make us in all colors!
Add flowers in all different colors. The snakies like it!

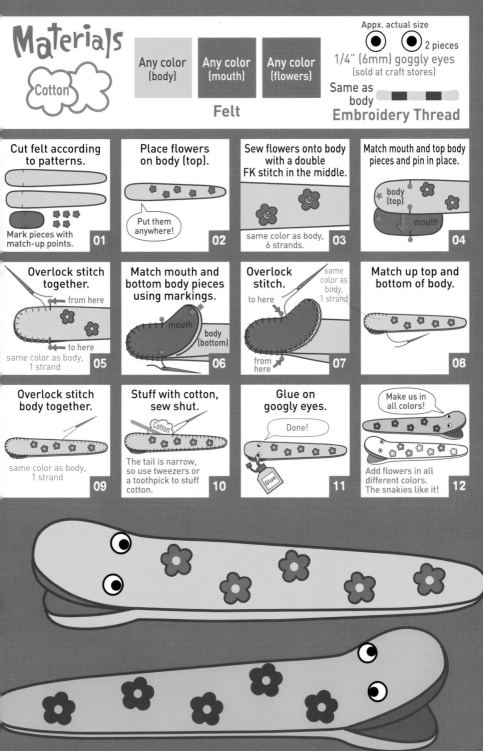

29

Bongo Bear Bunny

We know "Bongo" is a weird name to have, but that's our name! We're Bongo Bunny and Bongo Bear. Please don't forget it!

Patterns

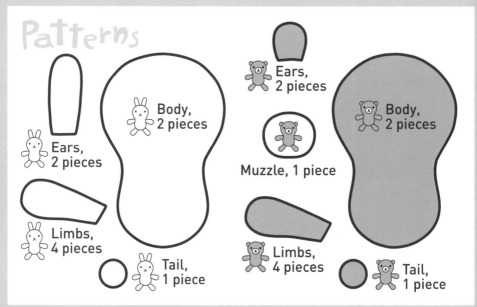

Ears, 2 pieces

Body, 2 pieces

Ears, 2 pieces

Body, 2 pieces

Muzzle, 1 piece

Limbs, 4 pieces

Tail, 1 piece

Limbs, 4 pieces

Tail, 1 piece

Materials

Cotton

Felt
Brown | White

Embroidery Thread
Brown
Black
White
Dark Brown

01 Cut felt according to patterns.

02 Cut felt according to patterns.

03 Eyes: Triple FK stitch.
dark brown thread, 6 strands

04 Nose: Double FK stitch.
dark brown thread, 6 strands
Mouth: S stitch

05 Eyes: Triple FK stitch.
black thread, 6 strands

06 Glue on muzzle.

07 Nose: Double FK stitch.
black thread, 6 strands
Mouth: S stitch

08 With limbs in between, overlock stitch around body.
white thread, 1 strand
brown thread, 1 strand

09 Stuff with cotton, sew shut.

10 Glue on tail.
Done!

Cloppity

Cloppity looks mean.
Cloppity has bad posture.
Cloppity has a bad personality.
Cloppity is a horse.

CLOPPITY CLOPPITY CLOPPITY CLOPPITY

Patterns

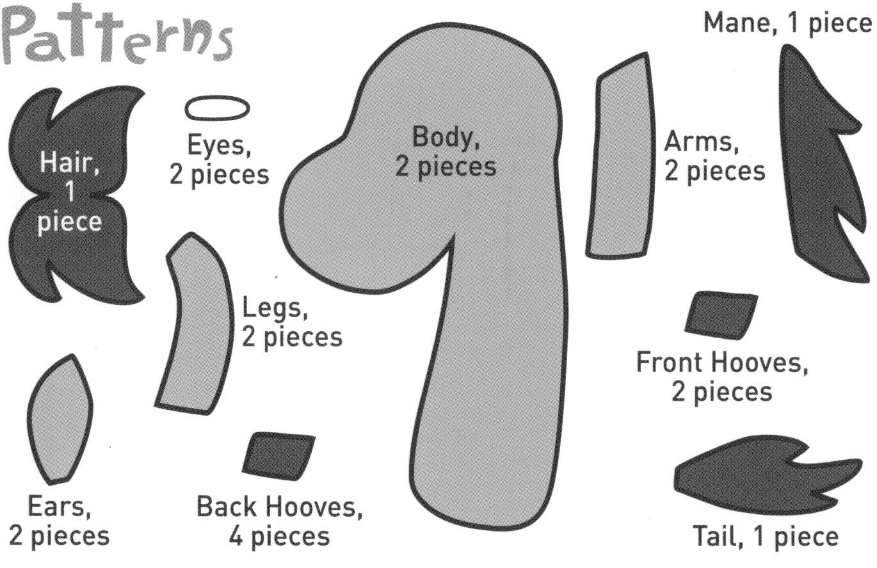

Hair, 1 piece

Eyes, 2 pieces

Body, 2 pieces

Mane, 1 piece

Arms, 2 pieces

Legs, 2 pieces

Front Hooves, 2 pieces

Ears, 2 pieces

Back Hooves, 4 pieces

Tail, 1 piece

Materials

Cotton

Felt: Light Brown | Brown | White

Embroidery Thread: Light Brown | Brown

01 Cut felt according to patterns.

02 Glue on eyes. Both sides!

03 Eyes: Double FK stitch. Brown thread, 6 strands. Both sides! Nose: Single FK stitch.

04 Mouth: S stitch. Brown thread, 6 strands. Both sides! Glue the underside of the thread and curve into a grin.

05 Place ears, mane, tail and legs. Lightly glue parts into place to keep from moving. Stack the ears. Glue

06 Overlock stitch around. light brown thread, 1 strand

07 Stuff with cotton, sew shut.

08 Cross-stitch arms onto body. light brown thread, 1 strand

09 Glue on hooves. Both sides! Glue

10 Glue back hooves onto both sides of feet. Both sides! Glue

11 Cut clefts into hooves. Front, too! With clefts, they look more like hooves!

12 Glue hair onto head. Glue it on like a wig.

13 Done! Neigh!

33

Penguin

Penguin likes cold places.
Penguin likes cold things.
But Penguin also likes flowers
and long springtime walks.

Patterns

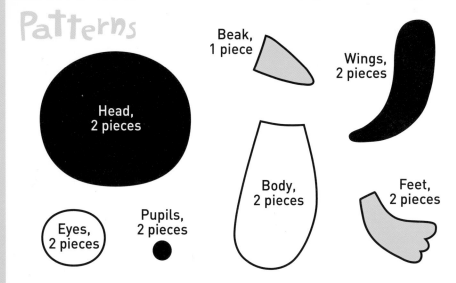

Beak,
1 piece

Wings,
2 pieces

Head,
2 pieces

Body,
2 pieces

Feet,
2 pieces

Eyes,
2 pieces

Pupils,
2 pieces

Materials

Cotton

Black | White | Yellow
Felt

White
Black
Embroidery Thread

Cut felt according to patterns. 01

Place eyes. white thread, 1 strand. **Cross-stitch.** 02

Glue on pupils. Oh! Both sides! 03

Place feet. Lightly glue in place to keep from moving. 04

With feet in between, overlock stitch around body. from here → to here ← white thread, 1 strand 05

Stuff with cotton. Cotton 06

Place beak. Lightly glue in place to keep from moving. 07

Place body. 08

With beak and body in between overlock stitch around head. black thread, 1 strand 09

Stuff with cotton, sew shut. Cotton 10

Glue on one wing. 11

Glue on other wing on other side. Done! 12

Try changing up the position of the eyes, wings and feet! 13

35

Fruits

Little strawberry, apple
and cherries make up
the Mini Fruit trio.
Make them in cute colors, okay?

Patterns

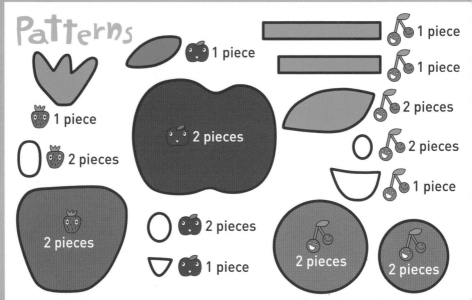

1 piece

1 piece

1 piece

2 pieces

2 pieces

1 piece

2 pieces

2 pieces

2 pieces

2 pieces

2 pieces

2 pieces

1 piece

2 pieces

1 piece

Materials

Cotton

Felt
- Any pink or red
- Green

Embroidery Thread
- Brown
- Green
- Pink or red to match

Strawberry

01 Cut felt according to patterns.

02 Glue on eyes.
brown thread, 6 strands
Pupils: Triple FK stitch.

03 Seeds: Single FK stitch.
brown thread, 3 strands

04 With leaf in between, overlock stitch around body.
pink thread, 1 strand
Stuff with cotton, sew shut.
Strawberry - Done!

Apple

01 Cut felt according to patterns.

02 Glue on eyes and mouth.
brown thread, 6 strands
Pupils: Triple FK stitch.

03 Overlock stitch around body. Stuff with cotton, sew shut.
red thread, 1 strand

04 Glue on leaf.
Apple - Done!

Cherries

01 Cut felt according to patterns.

02 Glue on eyes and mouth.
Pupils: Double FK stitch.
brown thread, 6 strands
Eyes: Single FK stitch.
brown thread, 6 strands
Mouth: S stitch.
brown thread, 6 strands

03 With stems in between, overlock stitch around body.
pink thread, 1 strand
pink thread, 1 strand
Stuff with cotton, sew shut.

04 With stems in between, overlock stitch around leaves.
Cherries - Done!
green thread, 1 strand

Panda Bear

Panda's not going, "Banzai!"
Panda's not doing stretches.
Panda's not saying, "I give up!"
Panda's just raising his arms. That's all.

Patterns

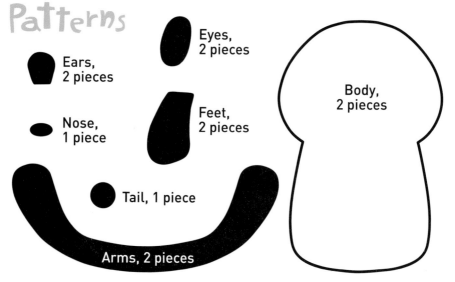

Ears,
2 pieces

Eyes,
2 pieces

Nose,
1 piece

Feet,
2 pieces

Body,
2 pieces

Tail, 1 piece

Arms, 2 pieces

Materials
Cotton
White | Black
Felt
White
Black
Embroidery Thread

Cut felt according to patterns. 01

Glue on eyes. 02

Glue on nose. 03

Mouth: S stitch. black thread, 6 strands 04

Place ears and feet. Lightly glue in place to keep from moving. Glue 05

With ears and feet in between, overlock stitch around body. white thread, 1 strand 06

Stuff with cotton. 07

Sew shut. white thread, 1 strand 08

Glue on arms (front). around here Glue front 09

Glue on arms (back). glue entire piece Glue front and back arms together. Glue back 10

Glue on tail. Don't forget! Done! 11

Sit Cat

We sit like good kitties. Mew!
But you have to take care when making us
or we won't sit properly. Mew!
Take care when making us!

Patterns

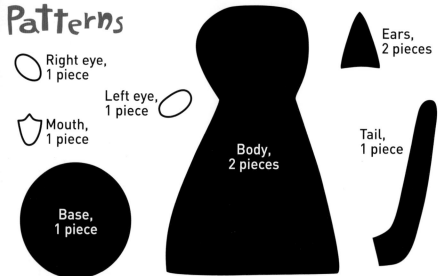

Right eye,
1 piece

Left eye,
1 piece

Mouth,
1 piece

Base,
1 piece

Body,
2 pieces

Ears,
2 pieces

Tail,
1 piece

Materials

Cotton

Felt — Any color / White

Color to match body — Embroidery Thread

01 Cut felt according to patterns.

02 Glue on eyes.

03 Pupils: S stitch. same color thread, 6 strands

04 Glue on mouth.

05 With ears and tail in between, overlock stitch around body. same color thread, 1 strand — to here / from here

06 Overlock stitch base to body. same color thread, 1 strand — base — Can you sew well, mew?

07 Stuff with cotton, sew shut. Back, mew! — same color thread, 1 strand — base — Done, mew!

08 With dark-colored kitties, white eyes and mouths stand out. Try making them in all kinds of dark shades.

09 With light-colored kitties, use a darker shade for the eyes and mouths. But they look a little scary. Still wanna try this, mew?

Rolleye Buddies

Our bug-eyes are always moving. Which is why it's hard to tell just what we're looking at. And since our eyes are always moving, you can't really tell what we're thinking.

Materials

Cotton

Various colors
Felt

To match
Embroidery Thread

For Penguin: 8mm (1/3")

Appx. actual size

2 pieces
1/4" (6mm) googly eyes
(sold at craft stores)

Raccoon Dog ① Cut felt according to patterns.

Patterns

Head, 2 pieces
brown

Ears, 2 pieces
brown

Mask, 1 piece
dark brown

② Glue mask onto head.

③ Nose: Double FK stitch. Mouth: S stitch.

black thread, 3 strands

④ With ears in between, overlock stitch around head.

brown thread, 1 strand

⑤ Stuff with cotton, sew shut.

brown thread, 1 strand

⑥ Glue on googly eyes.

Done!
Roll
Roll

Pig ① Cut felt according to patterns.

Patterns

Head, 2 pieces
peach

Ears, 2 pieces
peach

Nose, 1 piece
peach

② Glue on nose.

black thread, 3 strands

③ Nostrils: Single FK stitch.

④ With ears in between, overlock stitch around head.

peach thread, 1 strand

⑤ Stuff with cotton, sew shut.

⑥ Glue on googly eyes.

Done!

Bunny ① Cut felt according to patterns.

Patterns

Head, 2 pieces
pink

Ears, 2 pieces
pink

② Nose: Double FK stitch.

black thread, 3 strands

③ Mouth: S stitch.

black thread, 3 strands

④ With ears in between, overlock stitch around head.

pink thread, 1 strand

⑤ Stuff with cotton, sew shut.

pink thread, 1 strand

Roll
Roll

Done!

⑥ Glue on googly eyes.

Frog

Patterns

Head, 2 pieces
green

② Mouth: S stitch.

black thread, 6 strands

③ Overlock stitch around head.

green thread, 1 strand

⑤ Glue on googly eyes.

Finrib-bit!

① Cut felt according to patterns.

④ Stuff with cotton, sew shut.

43

Sheep

① Cut felt according to patterns.

Patterns
Head, 2 pieces black

Horns, 2 pieces white

② Cut along lines.

③ Place horns on 1 head piece.

④ With horns placed like this, overlock stitch around head.

black thread, 1 strand

⑤ Stuff with cotton, sew shut.

Done! Baa!

⑥ Glue on googly eyes.

Kitty

② Nose: Double FK stitch.

black thread, 3 strands

④ With ears in between, overlock stitch around head.

⑥ Glue on googly eyes.

Ears, 2 pieces dark pink

Patterns
Head, 2 pieces dark pink

pink thread, 1 strand

Done!

① Cut felt according to patterns.

③ Whiskers: S stitch.

⑤ Stuff with cotton, sew shut.

Bear

① Cut felt according to patterns.

② Glue on muzzle.

④ With ears in between, overlock stitch around head.

⑥ Glue on googly eyes.

Ears, 2 pieces dark brown

Patterns
Head, 2 pieces dark brown

Muzzle, 1 piece white

black thread, 3 strands

③ Nose: Double FK stitch. Mouth: S stitch

brown thread, 1 strand

Done!

⑤ Stuff with cotton, sew shut.

Dog

Patterns
Head, 2 pieces orange

② Nose: Triple FK stitch.

③ With ears in between, overlock stitch around head.

⑤ Glue on googly eyes.

Ears, 2 pieces orange

black thread, 3 strands

orange thread, 1 strand

Done!

① Cut felt according to patterns.

④ Stuff with cotton, sew shut.

Elephant

① Cut felt according to patterns.

② With ears in between, overlock stitch around head.
③ Stuff with cotton, sew shut.

④ Glue on googly eyes.

Patterns
Head, 2 pieces gray

Ears, 2 pieces gray

gray thread, 1 strand

Done!

44

Fox

Ears, 2 pieces yellow

① Cut felt according to patterns.

Patterns Head, 2 pieces yellow

② Nose: Triple FK stitch.
black thread, 3 strands

③ With ears in between, overlock stitch around head.
yellow thread, 1 strand

④ Stuff with cotton, sew shut.

⑤ Glue on googly eyes.

Done!

Panda

black — Ears, 2 pieces

black — Eye patches, 2 pieces

① Cut felt according to patterns.

Patterns Head, 2 pieces white

② Glue on eye patches.
black thread, 3 strands

③ Nose: Double FK stitch.
Mouth: S stitch.

④ With ears in between, overlock stitch around head.
white thread, 1 strand

⑤ Stuff with cotton, sew shut.

⑥ Glue on googly eyes.

Done!

Squirrel

Ears, 2 pieces light orange

① Cut felt according to patterns.

Patterns Head, 2 pieces light orange

② Nose: Double FK stitch.
Mouth: S stitch.
black thread, 3 strands

③ With ears in between, overlock stitch around head.
light orange thread, 1 strand

④ Stuff with cotton, sew shut.

⑤ Glue on googly eyes.
⑥ Draw on stripes with a brown colored pencil.

Done!

Alien

Ears, 2 pieces dark gray

① Cut felt according to patterns.

Patterns Head, 2 pieces dark gray

② Mouth: S stitch.
black thread, 3 strands

③ With ears in between, overlock stitch around head.
dark gray thread, 1 strand

④ Stuff with cotton, sew shut.

⑤ Glue on googly eyes.

Done!

Monkey

① Cut felt according to patterns.

Patterns Head, 2 pieces brown

Face, 1 piece peach

② Glue on face.
③ Nose: Double FK stitch.
Mouth: S stitch.
black thread, 3 strands

brown thread, 1 strand

④ Overlock stitch around.
⑤ Stuff with cotton, sew shut.

⑥ Glue on googly eyes.

Done!

Penguin

yellow — Beak, 1 piece

① Cut felt according to patterns.

Patterns Head, 2 pieces black

② With beak in between, overlock stitch around head.
black thread, 1 strand

③ Stuff with cotton, sew shut.

④ Glue on googly eyes.

Both sides!

Done!

Car Folk

What color is your car?
Make a little car in the same color.
Put eyelashes on the girl car.
Make them as appealing as you can.

Patterns

○ Eyes, 2 pieces

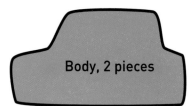

Body, 2 pieces

⬤ Tires, 4 pieces   ○ Hubcaps, 4 pieces

Materials

Cotton

Felt
Any color · White · Gray

Embroidery Thread
Black
Gray
Same as body color

01
Cut felt according to patterns.

02
Glue on eyes.

03
Pupils: Triple FK stitch.

black thread, 6 strands

04
For girl car's eyelashes: S stitch.

black thread, 6 strands

05
Mouth: S stitch.

black thread, 6 strands

06
Loosen the stitch to make a smile. Add a little glue to the back of the thread to keep in place.

grin

Use a toothpick to apply glue.

07
Add eye and mouth to opposite side.

Here, too!

08
Overlock stitch both sides of body together.

same color thread, 1 strand

09
Stuff with cotton.

10
Sew shut.

same color thread, 1 strand

11
Lightly glue on tires.

reverse · Glue · Apply here.

12
Cross-stitch tires to body.

gray thread, 1 strand

13
Glue on hubcaps.

Glue

14
Glue tires on other side.

Here, too!

Done!

47

sleepy Tetsu

Tetsu works at Aranzi Aronzo's shop.
And by "work" we mean "sleep."
He just sleeps all day long.
But that's his job.

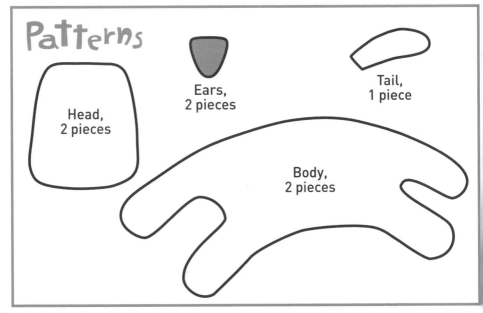

Patterns

Head,
2 pieces

Ears,
2 pieces

Tail,
1 piece

Body,
2 pieces

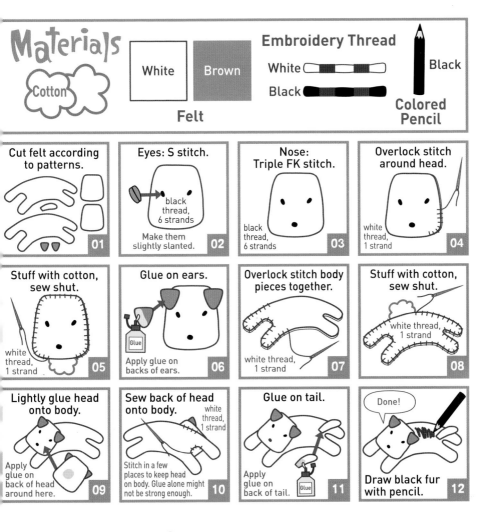

Materials

Cotton

Felt
White | Brown

Embroidery Thread
White
Black
Black

Colored Pencil

01 Cut felt according to patterns.

02 Eyes: S stitch.
black thread, 6 strands
Make them slightly slanted.

03 Nose: Triple FK stitch.
black thread, 6 strands

04 Overlock stitch around head.
white thread, 1 strand

05 Stuff with cotton, sew shut.
white thread, 1 strand

06 Glue on ears.
Glue
Apply glue on backs of ears.

07 Overlock stitch body pieces together.
white thread, 1 strand

08 Stuff with cotton, sew shut.
white thread, 1 strand

09 Lightly glue head onto body.
Apply glue on back of head around here.

10 Sew back of head onto body.
white thread, 1 strand
Stitch in a few places to keep head on body. Glue alone might not be strong enough.

11 Glue on tail.
Apply glue on back of tail.
Glue

12 Done!
Draw black fur with pencil.

49

3Piggies

It's the 3 Piggies, so make 3 pigs.
If there's only 2 pigs, they'd be the 2 Piggies.
And if there's just one pig, it'd be the 1 Piggie.
So please make all three.

Patterns

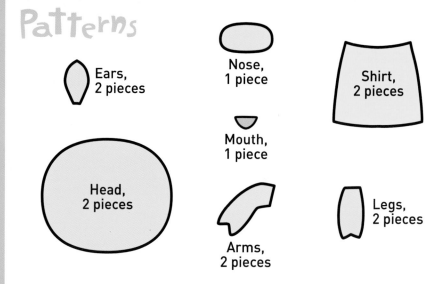

Ears,
2 pieces

Nose,
1 piece

Shirt,
2 pieces

Mouth,
1 piece

Head,
2 pieces

Arms,
2 pieces

Legs,
2 pieces

Materials

Cotton

Any color (shirt) — Peach — Pink

Felt

Peach — Black — Same as shirt color

Embroidery Thread

---

01 Cut felt according to patterns.

02 Eyes: Triple FK stitch.
black thread, 6 strands

03 Glue on nose.
Glue

04 Nostrils: Single FK stitch.
black thread, 6 strands

05 Glue on mouth.
Glue

06 Place ears.
Lightly glue on ears to keep from moving.
Glue

07 With ears in between, overlock stitch around head.
peach thread, 1 strand

08 Stuff with cotton, sew shut.
Cotton
peach thread, 1 strand

09 Place arms and legs.
Lightly glue to keep from moving.
Glue

10 With limbs in between, overlock stitch around shirt.
same color thread, 1 strand

11 Stuff with cotton, sew shut.
Cotton
same color thread, 1 strand

12 Sew head onto shirt.
Done!
peach thread, 1 strand

Make pigs with all kinds of faces.

13
Big nostrils: this pig snorts.

Tiny nostrils: this pig looks timid.

He's angry! A mean pig.

Big mouth: this pig's happy.

Make shirts in all kinds of colors, too!

14

51

Panda Bug

Panda Bug will listen quietly as you tell him your worries.
Take Panda Bug with you wherever you go so you can talk to him anytime.

Patterns

Ears,
2 pieces

Eyes,
2 pieces

Face/Back,
2 pieces

Matching
point

Tail,
1 piece

Black Stripes, 3 pieces

White Stripes, 2 pieces

Materials

Cotton

White	Black

Felt

White
Black

Embroidery Thread

Cut felt according to patterns.

01

Sew black and white stripes together in alternation.

① Stack a black and white piece together.

② Pin to keep from moving.

③ Overlock stitch top sides together.
white thread, 1 strand

Unfold.

④ Repeat with remaining stripes.

white thread, 1 strand

02

Fold stripes in half. Overlock stitch to create tube.

white thread, 1 strand

It's a tube!

03

Glue on eyes.

Glue

04

Nose: Double FK stitch. Mouth: S stitch.

black thread, 4 strands

05

Lightly glue ears in place.

Glue onto back of the face.

06

Sew back onto striped body.

Match arrow markings and sew.

white thread, 1 strand

07

Stuff body with cotton.

Cotton

Use a lot!

08

With ears in between, overlock stitch face onto body.

white thread, 1 strand

That was tough! Good work!

↑ Match arrow markings and sew.

09

Glue tail onto back.

Slightly above center.

10

Good job!

Done!

11

53

Haha Bunny

Haha Bunny is always laughing, "Ha ha!" If Haha Bunny wasn't always laughing, she'd just be a plain bunny.

Patterns

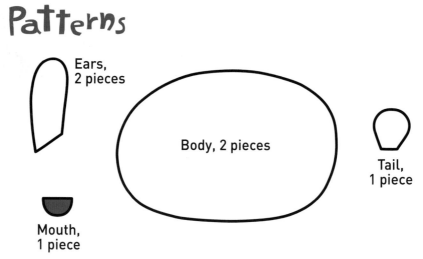

Ears, 2 pieces

Body, 2 pieces

Tail, 1 piece

Mouth, 1 piece

Materials

Cotton

White	Red

Felt

White ▭▬▬▬
Black ▬▬▬▬

Embroidery Thread

Cut felt according to patterns.

01

Left Eye: Triple FK stitch.

● black thread, 6 strands

02

Right Eye: Triple FK stitch.

● black thread, 6 strands

03

Glue mouth onto the left side.

Haha!

04

No mouth on the right side.

05

Place ears.

Haha!

06

Place tail.

Haha!

07

With ears and tail in between, overlock stitch around body.

Haha!

white thread, 1 strand

08

Stuff with cotton.

Haha!

09

Sew shut.

Haha!

white thread, 1 strand

10

Done!

Haha!

Left side

11

...

Right side

12

55

Lizards

Lizards' tails fall off easily, but they grow right back. So lizards with short tails will soon grow long tails.

Patterns

Legs, 4 pieces

Short-tailed lizard
Body, 2 pieces

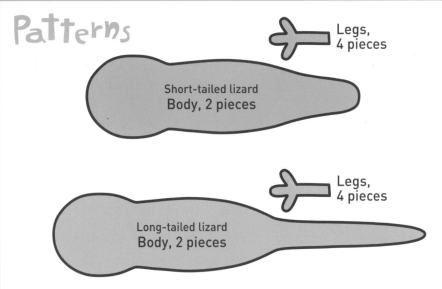

Legs, 4 pieces

Long-tailed lizard
Body, 2 pieces

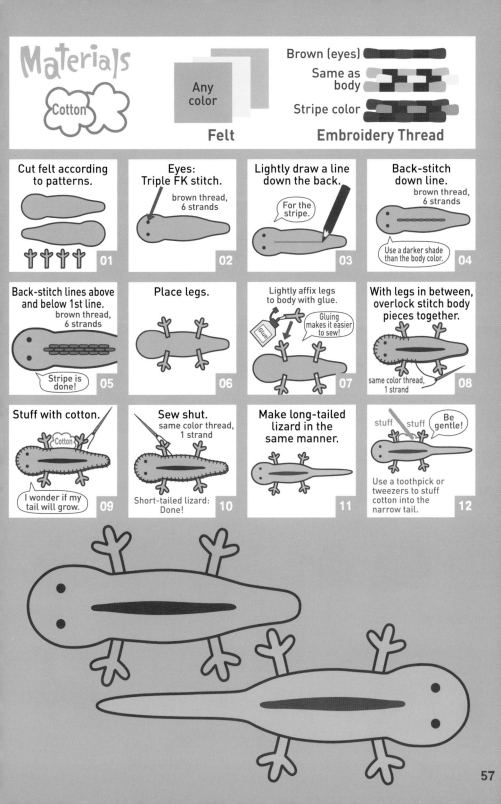

Materials

Cotton

Felt — Any color

Embroidery Thread
- Brown (eyes)
- Same as body
- Stripe color

01 Cut felt according to patterns.

02 Eyes: Triple FK stitch. brown thread, 6 strands

03 Lightly draw a line down the back. For the stripe.

04 Back-stitch down line. brown thread, 6 strands. Use a darker shade than the body color.

05 Back-stitch lines above and below 1st line. brown thread, 6 strands. Stripe is done!

06 Place legs.

07 Lightly affix legs to body with glue. Glue. Gluing makes it easier to sew!

08 With legs in between, overlock stitch body pieces together. same color thread, 1 strand

09 Stuff with cotton. Cotton. I wonder if my tail will grow.

10 Sew shut. same color thread, 1 strand. Short-tailed lizard: Done!

11 Make long-tailed lizard in the same manner.

12 stuff stuff. Be gentle! Use a toothpick or tweezers to stuff cotton into the narrow tail.

57

Chic white Rabbit

White Rabbit is a girly rabbit. She loves ribbons ♥, hearts ♥, flowers ♥ and plaid ♥. Make a cute dress for her, OK?

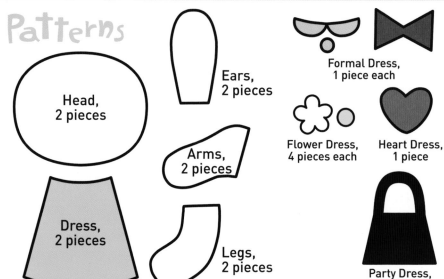

Patterns

Head,
2 pieces

Ears,
2 pieces

Arms,
2 pieces

Dress,
2 pieces

Legs,
2 pieces

Formal Dress,
1 piece each

Flower Dress,
4 pieces each

Heart Dress,
1 piece

Party Dress,
1 piece

Materials

Cotton

Any color (dress)

White

Felt

White
Brown
Same as dress colors

Embroidery Thread

Cut felt according to patterns.

01

Eyes: Triple FK stitch.

brown thread, 6 strands

02

Nose: Double FK stitch.
Mouth: S stitch.

brown thread, 6 strands

03

With ears in between, overlock stitch head together.

white thread, 1 strand

Stuff with cotton, sew shut.

04

After making a cute face, make a cute dress!

05

Formal Dress

Glue on collar and button.

Ear ribbon!

Glue collar on after attaching head to dress!

06

Heart Dress

Glue on heart.

Love is all!

07

Plaid Dress

Draw lines with colored pencil.

Trace over lines several times.

08

Party Dress

Pearls: Single FK stitch.

white thread, 6 strands

The dots are pearls, see?

09

Flower Dress

Glue on flowers.

Flower on ear!

10

Place arms and legs.

Lightly glue in place to keep from moving.

11

With arms and legs inside, overlock stitch dress together.

same color as dress, 1 strand

Stuff with cotton, sew shut.

12

Sew head to dress.

white thread, 1 strand

13

Did you make me a cute dress?

14

59

Alphabet

Make the letters of the alphabet, then spell your name, a message or anything you like.

Materials

Cotton

Any color

White

Felt

Black

Any color

Embroidery Thread

Cut felt according to patterns.

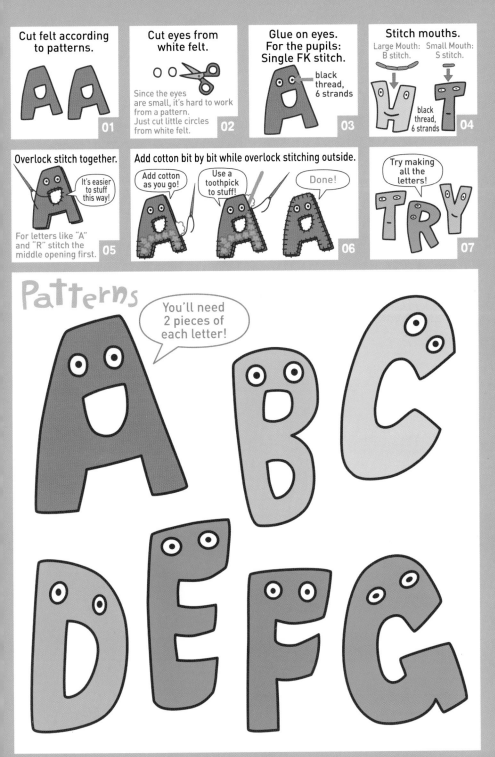

01

Cut eyes from white felt.

Since the eyes are small, it's hard to work from a pattern. Just cut little circles from white felt.

02

Glue on eyes. For the pupils: Single FK stitch.

black thread, 6 strands

03

Stitch mouths.

Large Mouth: B stitch. Small Mouth: S stitch.

black thread, 6 strands

04

Overlock stitch together.

It's easier to stuff this way!

For letters like "A" and "R" stitch the middle opening first.

05

Add cotton bit by bit while overlock stitching outside.

Add cotton as you go!

Use a toothpick to stuff!

Done!

06

Try making all the letters!

07

Patterns

You'll need 2 pieces of each letter!

A B C
D E F G

Rein and Rudolph

Rein has a black nose.
Rudolph has a red nose.
They're both Santa's helpers.
They're busiest during December.
They both love snowball fights.

Patterns

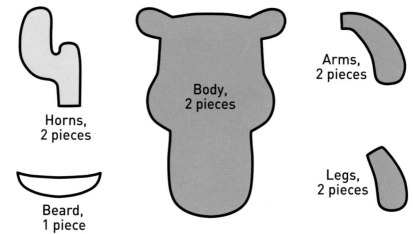

Horns,
2 pieces

Body,
2 pieces

Arms,
2 pieces

Legs,
2 pieces

Beard,
1 piece

Materials

Cotton

Brown	Light Brown	White

Felt

Brown
Black
Red

Embroidery Thread

01 Cut felt according to patterns.

This is for 1 reindeer.

02 Eyes: Triple FK stitch.

black thread, 6 strands

03 Nose: Double FK stitch.

Rein: black thread, 6 strands
Rudolph: red thread, 6 strands

04 Mouth: S stitch.

Rein: black thread, 6 strands
Rudolph: black thread, 6 strands

05 Place horns, arms and legs.

Lightly glue in place to keep from moving.

06 With horns and limbs in between, overlock stitch body together.

brown thread, 1 strand

07 Stuff with cotton.

08 Sew shut.

brown thread, 1 strand

09 Glue on beard.

Done!

10 I'm Rein.

11 I'm Rudolph. Can you tell?

Mr. Tree

Mr. Tree is a Christmas Tree.
A very tiny Christmas Tree.
A big Christmas Tree is good, but
little Christmas trees are fine, too.

Patterns

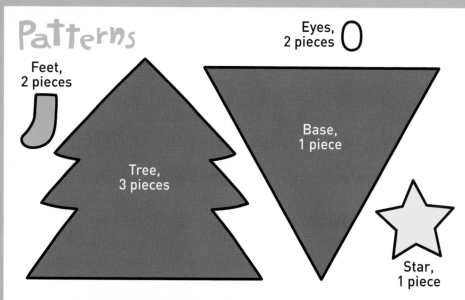

Feet,
2 pieces

Tree,
3 pieces

Eyes,
2 pieces

Base,
1 piece

Star,
1 piece

MERRY CHRIST MAS

Materials

Cotton

Felt
Green | White | Yellow | Brown

Embroidery Thread
Green
Black

---

01 Cut felt according to patterns.

A B ☆

C ○ ○

◖ ◗

---

02 Glue eyes onto piece A.

Glue

A

---

03 Pupils: Double FK stitch.

black thread, 6 strands

---

04 Draw zig-zag mouth with pencil.

---

05 Backstitch along zig-zag line. black thread, 6 strands

1 Out 2 In → 3 Out 4 In

5 Out 6 In → Zig-zag mouth: done!

---

06 Glue feet onto back of piece.

Glue

---

07 Stack A on top of B and overlock stitch right side.

to here

green thread, 1 strand

A ← B

from here

---

08 Place C behind A and overlock stitch together.

from here

C B A

to here

---

09 from here ← A

B C

to here

Overlock stitch B and C together.

---

10 Overlock stitch base to pieces A, B and C.

Feet in between

Base

---

11 Stuff with cotton, sew shut.

Cotton

---

12 Glue on star.

Merry Christmas!

Done!

---

13 Pretty colors!

Apple tree!

Make all kinds of trees for a fun Christmas!

You Can Do This

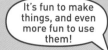

It's fun to make things, and even more fun to use them!

You can make cute yet useful things!

How to Attach Appliqués

① Add eyes, nose and mouth to the body.

② Place ears and legs under the body, then cross-stitch to whatever you like. (In this case, the ears and legs are sewn on under the body and head.)

③ Lightly glue on arms, then cross-stitch into place.

Try adding Rolleye Buddies to a small pouch. Little appliqués on little things are cute!

Add appliqués to a book cover. You can add appliqués to all kinds of things. It looks really cute!

Add Mr. Tree to a Christmas card. Very Christmas-y!

Paste Happy onto a Birthday card to make the Birthday boy or girl feel extra happy! Simply glue the felt appliqué onto card stock.

"My name is Kuma."
"Kuma" means "bear."
Spelling things out is fun.
If you use the alphabet appliqués, everything is easy to figure out.

You Can Do That

Cute hair bands and pins.
Sew hair accessories onto the
backs of appliqués.

"My bluebirds of happiness are right
here with me!"
If you sew little bluebirds onto safety
pins, you can add them as accessories.
Now you can take those birds of
happiness with you everywhere.

"Haha Bunny holds my scarf in place.
Now I'm super warm!"
Sew Haha Bunny to a safety pin to make a scarf brooch.

Enlarge the Sit Cat pattern by 300%
to make a big kitty. She's big
enough to look like a real cat!

A Turtlie pin cushion. Ouch!
If you stuff the shell with enough cotton,
a Turtlie makes a great pin cushion!

Make any
size you want!

Copier

Use a copier to copy the Patterns from
the book. Enlarge to any size you want!

You Can Do This

Make a Ghost finger puppet.
Pretty scary!
Even Liar is scared!
"Ack! Scary! Cut it out!"
Make Ghost,
but don't sew the bottom
and don't stuff with
cotton and you've
got a finger puppet.

Don't sew here!

I've got a snake ring!
Snake ring!
Totally cool!
If you make a really long snake,
you can even make a totally
cool snake necklace.

Try hanging a Polar Bear and Cub
from your handbag.
Sew a string to their backs so you can
hang them from the handle!

Give a Cloppity cell
phone strap to your
racetrack-loving
boyfriend.
He'll be thrilled!
Sew a cell strap to
Cloppity's back to
make a sweet
accessory.

This is not a Lizard that got squished by a book.
This is a Lizard bookmark.
If you don't stuff it with cotton and
simply sew shut you can make a Lizard bookmark.

You Can Do That

Make penguins in all different poses!
You can pose them in fun ways,
all by using the same patterns.

Give a Dharma doll to students studying for
a big exam. He'll cheer them on!
Glue on the other eye once the exams are over.
Write "Success!" on a piece of paper and
tape it on to make a headband.

Make a black car keyring
to match a black car.

How to Make a Keyring

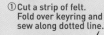

① Cut a strip of felt.
Fold over keyring and
sew along dotted line.

② With felt between
body pieces, overlock
stitch around.

It's a Munky Mobile!
Can you make a really long
Munky Mobile?
Make a whole bunch of Munkys
and hang each one's arm on
the next one's tail.

"Hey, Panda Bug, hear me out."
Panda tells Panda Bug what's on his mind.
Panda Bug will always sit quietly and listen carefully.
Panda Bug is always there to listen to whatever
you have to say.

71

ARANZI ARONZO

Aranzi Aronzo is a company that
"makes what it feels like the way it feels like and then sells the stuff."
Established in 1991 in Osaka. Kinuyo Saito and Yoko Yomura team.
Other than original miscellany, Aranzi Aronzo also makes picture books and exhibits.
Other books include *The Cute Book, The Bad Book, Aranzi Machine Gun vols. 1-3,
The Complete Aranzi Hour, Cute Dolls, Fun Dolls, Cute Stuff,* and *Baby Stuff.*

http://www.aranziaronzo.com

Translation — Maya Rosewood

Copyright © 2010 by Aranzi Aronzo

All rights reserved.

Published by Vertical, Inc., New York.

Originally published in Japanese as *Feruto no Masukotto*
by Bunka Shuppankyoku, Tokyo, 2010.

ISBN 978-1-934287-82-8

Manufactured in the United States of America

First American Edition

Vertical, Inc.
1185 Ave. of the Americas 32nd Floor
New York, NY 10036
www.vertical-inc.com